Other poetry books and chapbooks by Brian Bartlett

Finches for the Wake (1971)
Brother's Insomnia (1972)
Cattail Week (1981)
Planet Harbor (1989)
Underwater Carpentry (1993)
Granite Erratics (1997)
The Afterlife of Trees (2002)

Wanting the Day

Selected Poems
BRIAN BARTLETT

GOOSE LANE

Copyright © Brian Bartlett, 2003.

All rights reserved. No part of this work may be reproduced or used in any form or by any means, electronic or mechanical, including photocopying, recording, or any retrieval system, without the prior written permission of the publisher. Any requests for photocopying of any part of this book should be directed in writing to the Canadian Copyright Licensing Agency.

Cover photograph: "Geranium" © Lucy May, 2001. Reproduced with permission.
Cover and book design by Julie Scriver.
Printed in Canada by AGMV Marquis.
10 9 8 7 6 5 4 3 2 1

National Library of Canada Cataloguing in Publication

Bartlett, Brian, 1953-
Wanting the day: selected poems / Brian Bartlett.

ISBN 0-86492-357-0

I. Title.

PS8553.A773W35 2003   C811'.54   C2003-900516-X
PR9199.3.B374W35 2003

Published with the financial support of the Canada Council for the Arts, the Government of Canada through the Book Publishing Industry Development Program, and the New Brunswick Culture and Sports Secretariat.

Goose Lane Editions
469 King Street
Fredericton, New Brunswick
CANADA E3B 1E5
www.gooselane.com

For my first neighbours in poetry —
Alfie Bailey, Bill Bauer, Fred Cogswell,
Bob Gibbs, Travis Lane, Alden Nowlan,
Mike Pacey, Joe Sherman

I praise each day splintered down, splintered down and wrapped in time like a husk. . . . Time is enough, more than enough, and matter multiple and given. The god of today . . . unrolls, revealing his shape an edge at a time, a smatter of content, footfirst.
— Annie Dillard, *Holy the Firm*

Contents

From *Brother's Insomnia* (1972)
9   This Bridge Is No Bridge

From *Cattail Week* (1981)
10   Cattail Week
12   November Mare
13   In a House Where Chastity Was Taught for a Century
14   For Pauline Hooper of Eastport, Maine
16   Dark Scum

From *Planet Harbor* (1989)
18   Pillow on the Shore
19   Lost in the Margins
21   Bluegrass in Japan
24   River There, River Here
26   Cyclist's Diary: In the Tunnel
28   From the Upriver Bus
30   On the Bus from Beersheba
32   The Multiplication of Windows
34   A Distant Stream on Madonna Mountain
36   An Eft on Noonmark Mountain

From *Underwater Carpentry* (1993)
38   A Guestbook on Mt. Tillotson
39   Below Freezing on Montagne Coupée
41   Amphora of Wine 230 B.C.
42   Première Pédicurie
44   Museum Radiance
46   If Every Story Were Told Only Once
48   Weasel
49   Bear Bell
51   If I Knew the Names of Everything
52   Hotel of Dust
54   Kissing in the Carwash
56   Feast
57   Cousin Gifts

58 The Hands That Soap the Old Russian's Back
59 Diminished
60 Long Distance and Bleach
62 Underwater Carpentry

From *Granite Erratics* (1997)
72   A Basement Tale
74   An Imp Tale
76   A Drum Tale
78   A Best-Man Tale
80   A Skater Tale
82   Skylight
83   Always
84   Granite Erratics
86   When the Drummer Throws His Sticks Aside
88   The Uprooted Sleuth
89   Needy Space
90   Thanksgiving in an Old House
92   The Woods on the Way to School
100 A Sliver of Dawn

From *The Afterlife of Trees* (2002)
101 Under the Old Roof
104 The Afterlife of Trees
105 A Toss of Cones
106 Sloth Surprises
108 From *Talking to the Birds*
112 A Lake Named After My Ancestors
113 After the Age of Parties
115 Every Lion Until Now
116 A Glosa for Joshua
118 Sick for the New Millennium
120 Lost Footnote from an Essay on Rhythm
122 Foot-doctor for the Homeless
124 The Sonographer
126 How Acupuncture Is Like Poetry
127 Listening on the Back Steps

129 Author's Note

This Bridge Is No Bridge

pollen sinks through air onto water,
the stream so shallow
submerged branches could be shadows
of hackmatack reflections
where patterns match patterns:
            this bridge is no bridge
but a flowering over a flowing, hawkweed
and vetch sprawling where ruts
once filled with rain   dead blue lichen
blows off the railing, which has
warped and warped again,
its nails rusted and pinched

the forest loses in itself
eggs, excrement, antlers
though we found something
where trees are so close
we could climb two at a time:
            among choked roots we found
the dry ball of bones
an owl had burped up,
many histories locked together

in morning's bright haze we see
secondhand   we see
the dozen dances
but not the dancers:
            not water-striders
but water-strider shadows
flick and sway
across the clear underwater sand

Cattail Week

1

Hay fever traps him in the hot car
while she wades in shallow slime water.
Blackbirds want the red bandanna in her hair.
Lazily he watches her bend again and again.

Sleeveless, smooth-armed
she hugs twelve cattails into
the tall brown jug by the fire.

For a week the cattails
fatten — or does only he
see this?

2

Crazy man, she says (a sprig of
blue lupine between her
teeth), tempt me, throw
me one. I'll smash it open.

He gives her a wink and a cattail.
Time for a fandango. She swings the stalk
over her head, bends it round her neck
and into their faces

breaks a soft storm.

3

She lifts the jug onto her head and
leaps, lace slips off the table,
he spins, strikes one on brick as she
tramps on another, hurls it high ha
ha, cloudy seed swirls, spills, floats
over furniture, clings to hair,
mouths spit fluff, feet slip, his heart
hesitates as he sneezes the finest
sneeze of his life, snaps another over
his knee gently now while she
flings one against the ceiling where it
billows . . .

4

They look at each other across
the room, crouched, a couple of blackbirds.

November Mare

Our first snow in seven months
rises to the tops of a mare's hooves,
covers harness marks on her neck.

Dirty white, she is piebald with snow.
She stands still until the wind drops
and a red barn returns from the storm.

Down the mountain of her back
she begins to move: one hind hoof
nudges the settled flakes.

Her tail is a spread blonde plume
as she swings that hoof
digging down to a gnarled weed.

By now she knows the field
has withered from fence to fence
yet she goes on switching from leg

to leg, kicking clear
four circles of dead grass,
brushing the stalks with her lips.

When her head dips
low, she hears a thrashing underground —
Summer, a colt buried alive.

In a House Where Chastity Was Taught for a Century

In a house where chastity was taught for a century
a bastard son sleeps between his grandparents
in a bed hardly wide enough for two.
Ornamented with headboard horses, his crib
split last night under his kicking. Now
his mother's blossom scent is fainter
than the musk of the hound on the rug.

By this pale hour in the nearest town
she has left her walls of bright posters.
Gas-station girl, she wears the standard skirt
which rides up her legs as she stretches
over a windshield, or bends to a tank.
The boy who led her down basement steps
has gone like a cough in the night.
While she lifts a nozzle, a man by the car
traces her with his eyes, she squints
at his zippered jacket and wants again
the basement smell, the mattress wet as moss,
a warm face burrowing into her neck . . .

By a house where chastity was taught for a century
wind shakes the field of vegetables.
Dresses ashamed of knees and shoulders
long ago turned into rags on hangers.
Ancestors who saw cloven feet on dancers
tap their bald heels in the grave too late.

Heavy with pollen, wind crosses the yard,
climbs the window and laughs
at the grandmother slipping her arm
around the waking child.

For Pauline Hooper of Eastport, Maine

Scattered among stones and sand,
spikes torn from blood-streaked floors
join nothing to nothing,
staining the beach with rust. All
throbbing machines of your youth,
all canneries but one waste
away, blocky shapes under water and
ropes rotting back to their threads.

Each day that stink worked into your hair,
fish tails flew from your hands —
hands that tenderly shaved the face
and washed the back of Garnet,
stone below the neck half his life.
"Darling barber, don't I make you tired?"
Clutching a spoon you fed your husband
stewed tomatoes and cheese custards.
"Darling cook, why don't we dance?"

Crocuses around his grave drip in fog.
At a captain's desk salvaged from a ship
you struggle to write your sister.
Through a shuddering window
waves loosen slumped peers, wind
knocks bricks from chimneys,
storefronts are blinded with boards
where majorettes once lifted smooth knees.

Asleep, you're spared hearing
                                      your walls shift
though next door a child sees a dark, sleek thing
crawl from a shed and scuttle up Water Street.

Open your eyes only when the wind
stops bending crocus stems,
that child stops crying, and dawn brings
the restless sea —
Garnet rocking his head on a blue pillow.

Dark Scum

Wander down Water Street
past a headless weather vane,
signs eaten by fog, collapsed

stairways and porches,
barnacle-hooded rocks and
logs charred in old fires

to a broken-backed pier.
Purple and lime life
feathers the nearest wood,

followed by bareness
stretching out to the end
where dark scum clings.

Dark scum clings
where nobody, not even
the wildest child or dog,

sniffs or plays anymore.
Dark scum looks nameless
even in Latin.

Gulls veer away
to pick at anything else —
fish head? carrion rat?

Excrement of the wind or
fleece of a freak creature
who withered at the pier's end,

it has never been abandoned,
it has always been alone.
Eyeless, bodiless, blossomless

it stretches and threads itself.
Here where no voices reach
you want to paddle out

in some sturdy boat and
brush a hand over there so
look! it lives under your fingernails.

Cattail Week

Pillow on the Shore

A clam-picker's transistor
scares sandpipers with the news,
a patch of white suddenly
flashes at my feet —
                      blotched and ripped
softness, fringed with lacy blue.

What wind or flood swept it here
where nobody opens picnic baskets or
builds fires? What ear last pressed
against it, what greasy hair or neck?
What head laid its burdens down?

While that smooth voice from afar
sums up stricken lives, my words
less than feathers and cloth,

I lift my find into my arms, smell
dim origins, a promise of comfort.

Why does this surprise
                      hold my eye?
Long after blackness has climbed
above the sea, who will carry it
homeward, to a homeless stranger
shifting his head on rock and brick?

Lost in the Margins

Lost in the margins of this library book
someone has sketched bold skulls,
intricate skulls: mouths like empty

wells, eye sockets like vortices
spinning to fine points of pain.
Who are you, fellow reader? What

drove you at a crowded public table
or at home, behind a locked door,
to press the pencil so hard? Are you caught

in those sockets? Are you filling
other margins with other skulls,
x-rays of breathing men and women

stripped of flesh, all their evil
bared, layered like a tree's rings?
Do you ever rest a while, then draw

Yorick's skull, the face recalled with love?
The Hamlet in my mind doesn't
stand straight-backed holding the skull

aloft in the light, or lean
one way brooding, keeping
it at arm's length — this Hamlet

stretches out on earth, curled
at the edge of the gravedigger's pit, fondly
addressing the remnant cradled

Planet Harbor

in his arms. *He hath borne me on his back
a thousand times* says the Prince, on the level
with grave dirt, untheatrical,

hesitantly tapping the jester's skull.
Before the pencil breaks, add that
to the margins, every detail clear.

Bluegrass in Japan

1

A Canuck who's never set foot in Kentucky
    plays fiddle fast in Nagasaki.
Stooped like a heavy sunflower:
Abigail, the bassist.
They fly through "Mt. Fuji Breakdown."

   Spin the globe. Come back
to my kitchen, smell candle wax, hear
Schubert's quintet direct our forks
to the mushrooms and steamed salmon.
(I love your faded second-hand skirt
more than ruffled Viennese sleeves.)

Later, let's track down Thoreau's page
where words echo across a frozen pond,
shouting townsmen axing ice
to be shipped to Bombay and Madras.

2

Once the post office brought the seven seas
to my door. Avuncular tourist bureaus
    filled my hungry arms
with savannahs and castles and islands,
strange-scented paper from distant woods.

In a bright dream, I was there again
reaching up to a black lid:
envelopes of all sizes
stacked up to my chin, overflowed

onto the rug, and yet more dropped —

infinite answers, a bottomless mailbox.

3

Curiosity nearly kills the fox
   slipping through gardens, fleeing cars.
Glued to grape crates broken in an alley
the hills of Chile smell mysterious.
As he lingers, sniffing, headlights
leap into his eyes like two bursting suns.

   At twilight a shivering fisherman
forgets hunger for now,
                     kneels in moss to watch
a nuthatch climb down trees
head first —
         tricks new to his eyes.

4

Morning buoyed by a mandolin.
Satoko and Toshiko cheer,
cheek to cheek in the grass.

   All the rednecks in the rhythms
tug up their britches and
disappear:
        here no banjo strings
tighten around a slave's neck
or tie him to a tree.
               At last, at last, the music
climbs and soars, winged and free.

Wanting the Day

5

Walden's ice melts, the fox kicks up earth
catapulting decayed leaves. Day ends
with everything finding a new home —
you in my arms, play in a lyric, bluegrass in Japan.

River There, River Here

Afoot, two-wheeled, four-wheeled, I traced
that force towards its end, its overlap
with this planet's highest tides, slipped

southward & clung to changing blue,
no saint needed, no St. Tom or Dick or
John, no name like a stake stuck in earth

but a name flowing like those
hung, fluttering, above the tributaries (itself
a word riverish & akin to *Kennebecasis,*

Madawaska, Washademoak), sinuous &
fluent, thistles on the sandy banks &
violets on the loamy banks, log-jam scraps

trapped in shallows, their wet rot
stinking nicely near belle islets
hazed in silver, an osprey nest

the solidest thing in sight, great assertion
clumped at a tree top, vanished riverboats
buoyed by accordion tunes, my days

falling from the stalk like all the days
before my birth, the first pioneers'
first morning beyond reach, hopelessly

beyond reach, & how many visitors
called themselves the first, dogged
by insects & reflected light, map-makers

or worshippers of mapless gods
under circling stars, I following
no signs or arrows pointing, I now

climbing subway stairs a time zone farther
into the continent, sensing
if I turned around fast enough

here it would be at my back: a river
here like my cycling helmet
clinging long after I tugged it off

& hung it on a hook near the door —
that memory rushing into this moment,
this good pressure round my temples & ears.

Planet Harbor

Cyclist's Diary: In the Tunnel

1

A foolish turn, then swallowed up
by chilling monotonous dark.
Sound was one massive moan.

Far ahead, two tail-lights
faded — short-lived stars.
Home of no drifted seed, a breath-

less, gutted space, a naked cave.
No lit sign. No stick men. No
leaping red or white word.

2

Traffic-deafened, kept moving — a mole
lost and wild in a drainpipe.
Have never asked for dewdrops

suspended from every weed, sunlight always
glancing off my spokes, beauty
caught with every heartbeat; yet

sweating through that sudden
cold, through that trapped
howl, only felt loathing for that

skull scraped clean of all thought.

3

Bent by panic, began to fill
that emptiness with my eyes.
Where had the sky gone? Whispered

bits of history to blank walls:
*When the great basilica was finished
Ivan smiled at blue and golden walls*

*and blinded his architect.
As a peaceful man, a sweet-tongued lord,
he would've been "Ivan the Miserly"*

*for that single act, that heresy:
"Gold multiplied is gold subtracted.
A splendid bird steals its twin splendor."*

4

A spot of blue ahead. My heart in
the pedals, my bike parted the dark.
Dead space, awakened, stirred my hair,

my damp t-shirt. In a tunnel of nothing
couldn't imagine a glut of beauty.
That spot of blue grew like an iris

as eye-bandages are pulled off.
Sunlight rippled on handlebars.
The mole fell out of the drainpipe

and rubbed its snout in the familiar dirt.

From the Upriver Bus

1

At a steering wheel wide as a ship's wheel
he sits high, comically small.
Unknown others drone downriver, bearing
lumber or livestock, furniture or oil.
His hand, a winter-wrinkled leaf,
floats up toward the windshield.

His hand held up — not for a holdup
with a pistol, but for a greeting
unpremeditated as a kiss — brings him
no cheque, no deer meat, no
rainbow-papered gift on the doorstep.

Like a lone birdwatcher saluting another
if neither thinks he owns the meadowlark, like
a swimmer flinging one word in mid-lake
to a stranger swimming from the facing shore,
he hardly thinks of the gesture he makes.

2

When this river country was broken
by a trail a storm could erase, a man
with frost-hooded eyebrows sped along
in a sled, his family half hidden in fur.
Bells of a stranger's horses
became clearer and clearer.
Gloved hands, calling forth their imminent
gestures, slipped free of reins.

Struck by great waves, two ships warning
or threatening each other
startle the dark with blinking light.

   3

Though early today his bones cried out,
he waves his unmistakable wave
as long as the sun stays above the trees.

Only when no hand answers
from behind the other windshield
does he wonder why he lifts his hand at all.

Planet Harbor

On the Bus from Beersheba
December 1986

This narrow road keeps climbing,
I keep thinking *We're rising
into Jerusalem*,
              but no one looks impressed:
a boyish soldier with a *kippah*
atop his sweat-gnarled hair,
a purple-shirted Arab beside him
both gaze into neutral space. Even to my love
this trip is familiar.
Clutching my hand, she sleeps, she
sleeps as we rise into Jerusalem.

My eyes shut, why do I feel
we're aimed for a kingdom of clouds
where no lamb gets lost? My eyes open,
why do I wonder if this road will climb
for a week, a year?

The soldier's rifle glibly sticks
into the aisle. Exhausted
he starts nodding, nodding
sideways towards the purple-shirted
stranger. Slack-mouthed, he slumps
violently, almost dropping
his head hard onto the other's shoulder.

Rising into Jerusalem, I would flee
all imagery, rest in the simplest
splendor — a city fertilizing
its fair share of centuries,
a warm golden abstraction.

Wanting the Day

The soldier nods again, knocking
his blue-rimmed *kippah* crooked, the bobby pin
pulled loose, then drowsily, drowsily —
all strength fading from his neck —
his head hits the purple shoulder
once, twice, and I
turn away again, unable to watch.

The Multiplication of Windows

To a college girl jogging on Mt. Scopus
the Dome of the Rock was a common thing,
an old doorknob in the sun-stained distance.
Greeting her, I turned the word *stained*
over in my mind:
                    the blood of a stranger
knifed near the Jaffa Gate
soaking his shirt, streaking stones
pounded by generations of sandals;
   or light and colour rushing together
in Chagall's twelve windows: Reuben's cerulean,
Levi's drained yellow, Gad's malignant red;
Benjamin's mauve lion and multicoloured planets.

A rug merchant with fingerless gloves
bartered the life out of me, the price war
sportive. "Jerusalem my city —
my family live here
sixteen centuries — Jerusalem my city,
nowhere else —"
                  no rug for me
but new eyes on my own history,
what seemed so thickly woven
so thin
in the end: hardly three centuries
on the continent of lakes I call home.
      If my father's namesake, the Pilgrim Bradford,
had pointed the ship eastward and
cut adrift dreams of spruce and fir
for olive and oleander. . . .

Jerusalem, a solar system.
In one week, Jerusalem stained me.

Kicking a path at the woods' edge, half blinded
by fresh Quebec snow, I now find
windows within me:
                        a merchant unrolling
a rug; two cats tearing into garbage
on the Via Dolorosa; a Physics text abandoned
where prophets prayed that water spring forth.

As I squint into the heaped snow
those windows go black,
                        then light up, stained
with glacier-carved hills, deer tracks
leading down to lakes shaped like feet and eyes.

Planet Harbor

A Distant Stream on Madonna Mountain

Mist is wisping or scudding or slipping
over black-streaked slopes, under
amassed clouds; but dullness

spawns surprises here in the heights,
valleys & ridges hidden & revealed
in drifting, switching rhythms

no cloudless day includes within
its fixed vistas & strict forms.
Even on Madonna Mountain, who's pure enough

to stop comparing? Take two trees, two
chairs or saxophones or pig snouts, & sure as
rain sluices down the mountainside

we flick our eyes back & forth: a bold
bright day; a day of mists roaming or
gathering, mists our eyes choose over

this stern rock and that (luckily)
inflexible shrub you clutch —
you with your legs I've kissed

but never compared to each other,
you suddenly turning the kitchen
into a realm of laughter, hungry

& hungered after, uncatchable in sketch
or still life, your hands tracing
gestures clearer than falling water

or those windblown mists. Another day
our eyes alit, unexpecting, on light
casting across a pale slab

a lush fern's shadow like a deeply-
printed fossil, then a breeze played
over the fern, so the fossil

trembled, alive. All day we climb up
& down tricky slopes, threaded
to a racing millipede, a sailing wingseed

& whatever else moves. Thirsty, I say I hear
a distant stream — you say the sound
comes from your backpack, water

splashing inside your canteen.

An Eft on Noonmark Mountain

If winter winds shaved every twig
clean,
      if no frost-scarred leaf
still shook in high breezes
through sunlit freshets
before the slow explosion of buds,

this morning walk up Noonmark
would shrink a little,
            all these oaks
predictably stripped, the same in bareness.

Let them be, the leaves
that defied a season's savagery,
others amassed, moldering
at the feet of trees
        or blown far afield
into clattering brooks or across
silent deeryards,
        flattened further
by snow's chill and pressure.

Mark the patterns on Noonmark, here
and there:
      one hawk shrieking
at a pine's top, three warblers in an alder —
one winter pro, three migrators back
from florid Venezuelan riverbanks,
              their long flyways
theirs, theirs alone.

If no exceptions still clung to twigs,
if every insect lived
36 days (or 6 weeks),
                          if the pale green
baby ferns rising near my boots
                                all unfurled
together, right on time, presto, we'd be climbing
trails timed by Swiss watches,
and you could count me out — you
could shut me in a bare room
empty even of waterfalls on calendars.

Long as an infant's finger, an amphibian
crosses mossy ground,
                       a ray of light
needling its old-cheddar-orange back:
two or three years of this
squirming on forest floors,
                            then a return trip
to a brook, changing its colour
and habits (prince and pauper
rolled into one) —
                   but for now it
slowly scurries away
from my finger's shadow,
                         scurries:
shocked, vestigial-shaped, vivid.

Planet Harbor

A Guestbook on Mt. Tillotson

Armed with clippers and bowsaws
we left the first bootprints in months.
This morning we found six blowdowns,
made two cuts and heave-ho'd
each fallen one aside.
                        Collapsed from trees
melting snow hit the backs
of our necks, blended with the runoff.
Blowdown, walk-under, lean-to —
I loved that prepositional trail
leading over rock and spongy earth.

On the summit a spilled-over pond
rippled ominously close to our feet.
While beavers build systems of their own,
moose make use of our work —
their scats all over the trail
as if we were diggers of latrines.

In a shelter fragrant with damp wood
a scruffy plaid-covered book:
crammed with weather reports, complaints,
best wishes, quotations from the famous,
jokes; styles varied as trillium,
trout lily, yellow violet.
                        Pausing between
great gulps from his water bottle,
Allen recalled all the ignored blowdowns
across no path — outside our sight,
never our business: cryptic smudges
in the guestbook's margins. Bent
like a windblown tree, I wrote of them,

my words spring beauty, red lichen, skunk cabbage.

Below Freezing on Montagne Coupée

> *If every thousand centuries, says Buddha,*
> *a peacock feather is passed over a granite mountain,*
> *the day will come when the mountain will be*
> *eroded away and disappear.*
> — Kazantzakis, *Journeying*

A hidden river named L'Assomption
curves far below a thicketed
drop-off, and trees fine as eyelashes

fleck the horizon, beyond man-forsaken
barns up to their windows in snow.
A new decade, thermometers have climbed

past record highs all week
so skiing this morning I welcome
adamant air on my face, winter

winter again. Poling, kicking,
gliding — the closest I'll ever get
to being *lepus* — I'm propelled

past hare tracks and ice-encased
berries. In the corner store
last week, I heaped abuse

on the warm weather; at the scales
Mrs. Stavros said "And I thought
you were a nice person." Something

is slipping away, as if years
from now we'll no longer say
to everything there is a season

for everything will be
in every season, and our waxes
will end up back in the cupboard

Underwater Carpentry

shaved of a scant millimetre.
Rivière L'Assomption —
who or what has gone to heaven

leaving us here with our smoke
and defiled rain? No snow-goose feather
need erode this mountain

if roots and branches dry out
and drift free, soil runnelled
away, with nothing to hug.

A vole, stunned
by the darkness or chill
of my shadow falling across the trail

pauses, sniffs for bearings —
its heart rate astronomical —
then streaks into its tunnel

finished
with the one human stranger
of its short life.

Amphora of Wine 230 B.C.

Stern and bow were equally obscure
deep down where the sea
held one smudge of radiance —
a waterproof lamp
laying bare an earthenware amphora
wrapped in six species of shellfish.

Tell us, Cousteau and crew,
how at a great wooden table
you lifted embossed cups and
drank, falling through the centuries.
Was it bitter like a fruitless dive
or sweet like nitrogen narcosis?
Did you catch a trace of slaves'
blood — the human winepress?

Some of us are so eager to put
the past on our tongue
— even for one moment — we'll wait,
wait until you say you tasted
vanished cheese, midnight-black olives,
grapes picked under a vanished sky.

Première Pédicurie
            New Orleans, 1873

    1

After the birthday songs and paper birds
    sailed through the living room and crashed
into Mama's curtains, Josephine
    curled her toes inside her shoes, danced
down rain-slick streets, past coach horses
    crisply drumming their hooves —
every horse male, every dove female.

Lamplight spreads around her naked foot
    propped on a sheeted chair. Like many men
the doctor looks one-lipped, his moustache
    thick as a Siberian bear's fur. She fears
fingers cold as eels pulled
    from a murky creek,
                    then feels a touch
like Mama's limbered by bath water.

In rhythm with his shifting boots'
    quiet snapping, the doctor's scissors
shut like gentle beaks. Relaxing
    back against a cushion, she fully
trusts a nameless man's hands —
    the first, maybe last, time. Trimmed
nail by nail, she shivers up and down
    her spine and runs her eyes
up and down the room: cigar smoke smudging
    Papa and his brother from France,
mon oncle célèbre, le drôle de type,

two men, familiar but abstruse,
    a blue smell foreign as a horse's eyes.

42

Wanting the Day

2

She doesn't know Uncle Edgar's hands
    twitch with his sketching pencils' absence.
Bored by her Papa's talk of the cotton trade
    he notes her plain chemise and suddenly
untroubled eyes, and will not lift her
    among nymphs' tendrils and fountains
or banish the doctor. But if
    she finally cries out in pain
startling the dog napping near the men
    he will push her cry
back into silence, give it no colour.

His paints upstairs, his eyes reach
    through the smoke and hold what he needs:
a basin footbath, a sore-toed girl
    straight-backed and yielding,
a bald doctor snipping her dead skin away.

Museum Radiance
"man's hat, ca. 1740"
for A.G. Bailey

1

Impossible to touch without breaking glass,
black fur with earflaps
rests there, dumb — a castaway
in empty space. The lack of a story
becomes hard to bear. Waiting
I call forth farmers up the Nashwaak
reviving a tribal memory:

Before snowy wind flogged their coats
settlers barely raised simple shelters
in a clearing humble as a deer yard.
Lake ice grew too thick
for fishing holes, cold lips touched
hot foreheads, bits of bread soaked up
squirrel-meat grease. Diseases were storms
within storms. And the dead were hung
in the trees until spring, too frozen
for ravens, too high for wolves.

2

A hat under glass is a hat under glass
but I will not stop there.
Starving does, Scottish laments,
monstrous trees, the empty space ...

In spring, what a crop of burials!
Who had ever seen such pine cones?

Wanting the Day

In summer, children grappled up into
those trees, shouted across a valley
more tangled than any map,
licked sap from their hands.

One boy found his father's hat up there
and wore it for days, defied
the season. His cream-pale face
burned, the heat of play
like a January fever.

If Every Story Were Told Only Once

Suppose we were a tribe blessed with speech
untouched by triteness, some *lingua vernal*
like new species of insects born
daily in the pools and the tree tops, buzzing
something fresh each morning.

On the flat rocks by the beaches
children make up skipping rhymes
by the minute. Together fifty years
a man and a woman never need
to jab a stick at the fading coals
and sigh, bored by this tale or that.
Mangoes and vines and lizards
are lustrous with youth.

If every story's told only once
how do we listen?
                      If every joke,
tragedy, confession, has one chance
    do we panic
with the fear of daydreaming? Turn
your back, and lose forever
a wild boar darting through lamplight,
a meteor dissolving down the sky.

On the everblooming island
when we try to sleep
                    the day's dialogues
hang, tantalizing, out of reach.
Children cry, greedy to hear
a particular lullaby again

but the words and the tune
died in our mouths.
                    After midnight
we still go *hush*, desperate
to bring back the loved song.

Weasel

A boy started out through thick mist
while his family slept: vacation
on the farm, hours before the mill drone.
Past forbidden mountains of sawdust
he climbed a dew-drenched field.

Hiding the barn, mist tingled
his bare legs — then in a minute's quick
cycle, it rolled away as if the light
were wind,
        and the sun touched
every cluster of grass,
every fence post, bark spiral,
goldenrod spire, stone. In a silent
unmoving world,
        he suddenly faced
another one awake — a weasel
upright in a tractor print.

Between two breaths   it was gone.

The boy became a man with a weakness
for branches, webs, interweavings,
but then and even later he still
stood in a field with that other —

that tawny, singular one
        born from mist,
morning rising in both lit eyes.

Wanting the Day

Bear Bell

> *Whistle, talk, sing, or carry a noisemaker...*
> — Environment Canada, *You Are in Bear Country*

Fear turns around in my mouth
like sweetness, honey dissolving

or clogging the throat, caught —
Grizzled lodgepole pines cut

down the thin light further, murking
the trail. Ribboned to my knapsack

this tin bell does nothing but
declare me. A good citizen,

I washed away my aftershave
so as not to tickle your nostrils.

O Mama Jasper, hear how
one peaceful Sunday years ago

four provinces from here
a local grocer's steel-heeled son —

hot from family battles — crossed
the sidewalk I knew best,

planted his knuckles in my eye
because he had to strike someone

and I was someone; so ever since
on unremarkable nights

when a fiercely-striding stranger
approaches, I veer, ready

to flinch or fall. In a blink
that city panic vanishes — but not

this fear between mammals, this
mixed need and dread

of what I am not. However much
I want you to break loose

(no more a figment)
I thank the Great Bear above

each time a shadowed stump
turns out to be a shadowed stump,

a boulder a boulder. Then I hear
the jingling of some jester's bell.

If I Knew the Names of Everything

If I knew the names of everything
the depths of this canyon would rise
to the surface, these forests swallow
their own shadows.
                If I'd sniffed and kicked
every spot on earth, I wouldn't be holding
this torn map up in clear light, brushing
my eyes over rivers I'll never cross.

                Fun to bump into
a different species or two
a year, but praised be the biggest zoo
for being
small,
      just a neck — or toe — of the Woods.
Praised be the anonymous fish, the bird
free from all human eyes, the undiscovered
insect biting the rarest antelope's ear.

My boots at my side, I'm waiting
for the Maligne Canyon to turn
malign. Swollen by heat, my feet bathe in water
fallen from white peaks where bighorn
feed, cold climbing from my legs to my skull.

      If I'd spotted and tagged
every species, if I'd stared down
every sub-species, if every Sudanese
savannah, Arctic pingo, or Pacific reef
were home and native, I'd burn this map.

Flecked with heraldic gold,
  what winged thing has landed
    on my drying foot?

Hotel of Dust

1

Graceful on the Imax screen
                            a blue planet
was turning — mountains and seas
unfolded in light. Watching
who wouldn't think *Let me live
down there*. The theatre lifted me beyond
gravity. I hardly blinked,
afraid splendour would slip away.

  Blocks distant, in the lobby
of the All Too Real Hotel, a scabby hand
jumped from darkness,
                            rum-wet words
damned me: what a whirlwind
scorching the side of my face!

2

Winnipeg dogs me
with morning heat. The stink of carpets
wanders the halls, the bathtub
contains more history
than I'm willing or able to read.
In the fractured mirror I search
for the X on my cheek.

This isn't suffering; it's a holiday
with a well-creased map
open on a scarred dresser,
a minute in a hotel of dust.

Wanting the Day

3

Our planet's textures were stripped
down by distance, yet tinged
iris, cobalt, dust:
                like an infant
held near the dinner table, how I wanted
to touch them all, Mongolian
wastes, Uruguay, Baffin Bay.
                              Floundering
in shadows, back in the dank lobby,
that voice spat, cut.

"Fellow earthling" I might've begun
but he burned in that corner,
distant as Pluto, under a stopped clock.

.

Kissing in the Carwash

Sometimes light dims,
the onslaught of things
drives us from the wind

and the window
to each other's eyes. Forces
shake senselessly, we

can do nothing
to stop them. It's a liquid
world, awash with

fateful shapes
blundering
mechanically,

where we come to rest
like deep-sea divers
chained, our oxygen

running out.
For oxygen, good oxygen
my mouth goes straight

for yours, and it's a liquid
world, fuller than summer's
peak, the industrial thud

slowly fading
in our own lush wash
closer than home. We overlap,

more than over-
lap, we lap, we taste
good to each other, so

steal my breath, lickety-
split. My better lips, my
lap, you banish

all dross —
precious simplifier . . .
complicator.

Back in light's hard glare
my sight runs and leaps
thanks to your sight,

to my tongue's
dark red memories
of your tongue,

your close whisper louder
than the heedless waves
flooding around us.

Feast

One cob dropped into steaming water;
  then a thousand. Where sun, butter, corn
    were one another, how many cousins

flocked to the great tables, reaching
  for a third or fourth? It was August
    1989 . . . 1898 . . . 1719 . . .

Collapsed into tall grass with eyes
  closed, we dreamed we punted
    around a pond thick with spatterdock

bobbing above yellow perch. On our raft
  a sulfur-shaded caterpillar slowly
    ate a yellow-birch leaf

while grosbeaks dipped overhead
  and the smell of goldenrod blew our way.
    A dying, rabid fox in a cove

rolled in buttercups, smeared with waxy dust.
  When our dwindled vessel sank
    we found ourselves back in the grass,

the scattered cobs nude and old.
  Full, we retrieved the beginning:
    silky strands clinging to fingers,

empty husks tossed into a wooden box,
  and stoking our hunger further
    rhythms of a tough green tearing.

Cousin Gifts

The names of three dozen cousins shook
together in a hat. Our mothers always
chose the gifts, always wrapped them
neatly, with clean creases. Cousin gifts
were never revolved near lamps. Buried
under more promising packages, shoved aside,
they were the orphans under the tree.

One autumn your name wasn't put
in the hat, and you knew you were aging,
adrift in your teens.

Two decades later at Christmas, family news
gathers like darkness on shedding boughs:
Doris unemployed after ten years selling
train tickets, Wheeler's bank account emptied
by his fleeing wife, a fatherless child
born to Sylvie in high school, Donald
tongue-tied, on tranquilizers . . .

My cousins have scattered to Corner Brook,
Mississauga, Burnaby, New Guinea.
Some are happy, says my mother,
but those who aren't
I try hardest to recall — voices
drifting across a picnic table, breaking
a lake's calm in two; then only
their hands turning over and
over, eyes facing kitchen tiles.

My cousins . . .
I do not know what gifts to give them.

The Hands That Soap the Old Russian's Back

Ti-Doug cycles from home to home,
lifts the young and the old in their beds.
As he feeds and wipes paralytics,
far back in their eyes he sees
the chance-taking drivers that put
them there. A young priest refuses
to be wheeled to Mass again, his only flock
the sparrows on the windowsill
scratching seed. A 300-pound storyteller
offers an overflowing glass of gin
before the bathing begins,
the scar of a Red Army bullet showing
through white chest-hairs.

5 o'clock, exhaust fumes, Sherbrooke St.
lit like a car factory: Ti-Doug veers,
his mirrored shades breaking the cars
into shards. When a stranger
seizes space, cuts him off, he acts.
The hands that soap the old Russian's back
suddenly squeeze
a bicycle's brakes, tighten
into a fist, slam a Mazda's hood.

Rubber bat wings and spider
glued to his black helmet
shudder; in his knapsack a stained smock
lies folded like other wings.
His tires grind meekness away.

Diminished

The obituaries slide from my hands:
the man we mocked is dead.

At parties we heard his underthunder,
his sudden bray; glimpsed him
pinching women the old-fashioned way,
asking to have his hand slapped —
the bad boy, proud of it,
his hair gleaming like flaked silver.
Out of his earshot, we turned
words like "insufferable" into olives.

"Epicurean George": neither friend
nor enemy, expert on tax dodges,
pasta, Hawaiian hips and sarongs.
One night last January he vanished
into the climbing snow, then brought back
four bottles of saki from his car
and tried to make us all feel
it was our duty to drink.

The tumours took six months — insufferable.
The ink stating his birth and death
barely smudges my fingers. We try
the Japanese seaweed he praised — *nori*
floats like ashes over the soup.
The tongue of our mocking is still
and the wine tastes weaker than it did.

Long Distance and Bleach

Laundromats care nothing for readers,
   the shudder of machines break up
the words. I shut the book
   in my lap, look up: atop a dryer
a goateed stranger is meditating
   motionless in the lotus position;
a red-eyed old woman pours bleach
   straight from a bottle; a girl
yells into an unsheltered pay phone
   "My sister, I said I want my sister!"

Digging into a tight pocketful
   of coins, she rails at an operator
"Speak English" — trying to reach
   a number in T.O. — "or I'll smash
your face!" The woman with bloodshot eyes
   uncaps the bottle of bleach
again, holds it over the washer
   as if dousing a fire. "Not
another quarter!" screams the girl
   at the smeared, initial-scratched
phone. "I want my sister, Esther!"

I try my book again, but the voice
   doesn't stop, stuck between fury
and begging, and the old woman pours
   bleach from a bottle that seems
to have no bottom. How deep
   can a stain be? I counted on
a sluggish hour alone, but sense
   an uprising in the inner works
of strangers and machines; and inching
   toward the bench's edge,

expect hidden fires to gust
   from washer and mouthpiece
and we'll still be trying to reach
   our sister or brother
when the flames melt us all together. . . .

But who expects the world to end
   in a laundromat at 3 PM? The dryer
keeps on spinning under the man
   in the lotus position, and the girl
cries into the phone, "Is it you?"

Underwater Carpentry

A door blows open, a door blows shut
and nobody comes to adjust, the wind
propelling wrappers and newspapers
up Boulevard St. Laurent damp at night.

I wanted a poem without a time or place

but find myself wandering alone
in a suspended hour, where a barbershop
displays a stuffed wolf, its glass eyes
overlooking the aftershave. Who could ignore
a wolf in a barbershop, or the news
doing cartwheels around parking meters?

All the pages in my older paperbacks
yellow, and I look for that colour
in my eyes. Yesterday I swore off
scratching in the margins of books
since my library won't be buried with me
and someone will inherit.
   Albee forswonk and forswatt I am.

One show sold out,
               I'm a-roamin'
& a-ramblin' til the next
colliding with myself and my friends
new to these streets years ago
when every bookshop, café and bar
was festooned with hopes, and we plunged
into singalongs in the Cock'n'Bull
thinking the Irish had it all.

After Hermione kissed Leontes at last
and *The Winter's Tale* wound down

with the beauty of its speech —
   O she's warm!
   If this be magic, let it be an art
   Lawful as eating —
outside the theatre a spinning red light
struck us in the face. Two women kicked
and elbowed each other, screamed
"Voleur! Salope!" until the handcuffs'
decisive snap.
           I was so green
I smiled at the wedding of two worlds,
Elizabethan redemption
with the hard facts and the dying siren,
but gave no thought to the women's scars
or the keys in their pimps' hands.

Faces of politicians and models
jump from magazine window-displays
into the street. For some citizens
downtown is the other side of the moon.
Mrs. Feinstein, for one, never strays
from the leafy streets of Outremont,
the kosher bakery blowing the aroma
of poppy-seed cake out over the sidewalk,
her golden-branched menorah on lace.

Cold fell upon the pages of the Torah
one month as I handed her the rent:
the fortieth anniversary of the morning
she stood half-naked watching her family
disappear down a hallway
in Auschwitz.
           How would the Talmud
gloss the morning she wrung her hands
crying "My ceiling, oh my ceiling!"

since I'd left the washer tap on
all night? In her tidy kitchen I found
the faint moon of one bubble mark
overhead. Her sack of worries holds
snowy balconies, taxes, dirt, my footsteps.
I try to match up that day in '45
with the flawed ceiling
                          and go numb.

In these, the last months before books
will be taxed by the shoe
that governs us and kicks our words
aside,
      William Tyndale surfaces
from one of the yellowed pages.

"God's mattock" in London and Antwerp,
defiant fugitive, he would translate
until his fingers could move
no more. When a shipwreck sank
years of his work, he started again:
   If God spareth me life, ere many years
   I will cause the boy that driveth the plough
   to know the words better than I do.

I once heard a poet at a conference claim
she hadn't a drop of Wasp blood in her
capping off the proud fact "Thank God!"
and all we Wasps in the room
chortled, got out our little whips
and beat ourselves a bit.

In my childhood — one big Wasp nest —
in the shadow of the basement furnace

I would hear Jesus rustling nearby,
fear that he might touch my shoulders
with a mission. In the same era I'd stare
at Biblical posters over my hockey cards
and, turning over two phrases, whisper
"Son of God . . . son of a whore,"
straddling wordplay and blasphemy,
vaguely thrilled and guilty.

Under distant etched lightning
a woman in diaphanous white
and a man with a sheep's horn at his waist
hold a cape over themselves, escaping
into the world of grief. Before I ever
heard the Lord's footsteps near the furnace
that couple on my grandparents' wall
made me quickly turn away, dreading
the darkness and the storm
beating their cape. After Gramp's funeral
a generation later, I carted the painting
back to Montreal on the train. Restless,
suddenly fraternal toward the couple
in the storm, I dreamed of a sheep's horn
calling and calling in the night.

Heirlooms like that, then this trash,
so much trash blowing past
or glued to fences around construction sites
among anonymous messages:

LEGALIZE FREEDOM

    TRIGGER HAPPY GOLDFISH

PUKE UP 60s

REFUGEE EARTHLINGS

EARTH FIRST

VIVA HOLOCAUST

Earth first, you bet, wiser words
than those of the Ella Fitzgerald look-alike
who haunts the sidewalk under my balcony
singing gospel songs at the top of her lungs
until addressing the parsley and mint
in the Pakistani food shop, she growls
"The Mark of the Beast is on us!"

The air fails to stir; rain aches to fall.

Storefronts mask the inner-city church
where the World Saxophone Quartet hooted
and squiggled forth a holy racket, enough
to make the stained-glass prophets scowl
or smile, a joyful noise unto
the earth.
        When did the tide turn,
when did I finally feel
                the earth was my mother
(father) more than any Nameless One
was my father (mother)? Clues spawned —
the tidbit that our word *muscle*
evolved from the Latin for *mouse*
since rippling muscles reminded the Romans
of mice running under the skin.

More than the Holy Ghost muttering or whistling
along my bloodstream, those rodents
shrieked to be heard . . .

The P.O. has put the flying squirrel
on the 1¢ stamp: I'll free the beast
or at least up its value
   (*we* are the mark of the beast, Ella)
but the hypocrite (me) works
with a trio of Lansdowne's birds
framed over the computer:

the heron for reach and poise, the thrasher
for song and speech, the waxwings
for their plucking of berries
and passing them from beak to beak.

Two summers ago the drought out West
burned through the news — summer-long fire.
The night we sat with interlaced fingers
through the W.S.Q.'s squiggles and hoots
my love and I returned home to see
what we could do about the drought,

my long-fingered love and I colliding
in the night   ahoy   awake   make our mice
leap   prime the pump   drop the bucket
into the sweet well   drought? what drought?
make our fortune   irrigate the plains . . .

Then, leaping far back, I said:
   Atremble on a slick windowpane
      a sixteen-legged spider shifted and spread.
   No Galapagos reptile astonished Darwin more.
      Sketching a tangle of legs
   over airmail blue, I at eleven
      prayed *Wild World* in mythic London
   would call me the first, give me a spot
      in the annals of natural history.

Underwater Carpentry

Blunt, all too brief, the answer
　squashed my hopes; I couldn't grasp
it: a four-syllabled word starting "cop"
　(spiders on patrol?), me banished
to the scrubland, where two spiders kept
　shaking legs on a windowpane.
She laughed and we tangled our
four limbs into eight again.

The most flattering thing another woman
ever told me in our years together
was that my soul was like an accordion
unfolding, always surprising her.
But of course I stopped
surprising her.

I've wanted a poem that takes a few
flying leaps, a pineapple-rich mind, a voice
freed of all travels but those
inside. I've wanted a poem without
time or place, but the four elements
hold me hard, one way out
to sneak in many times and places:

　Glenn Gould conducting hippos at the zoo
then hunched at the piano stool, rapt
and bearing down on Bach;
　　　　　　　　　or Margie Gillis
on a floodlit bug-thronged stage, dancing alone
but dancing for many, changing
from young woman into old,
　　　　　　　　　old into young.

Some say orderly words are war-like
but I wonder if the metaphor's fair,
if the linear can also be the dive
of a swallow guided by a white feather
set prominently at the back of its nest,
million-year-old air-traffic control.

    DEATH MUTATION VENGEANCE

        PHENOMENAL DESCRIPTION

    RISE UP OR MELT DOWN

        THE DEADLY NIGHTSHADE IS WATCHING YOU

If we all danced on a bug-thronged stage
showing our best! Have other teachers
choked on course evaluations, felt
like Saint Cassianus stabbed to death
by pupils' pencils? I want to sing,
not judge or be judged. A poem
might become like an accordion
unfolding,
        or better to become un-
astonished, your calmness showing
the misshapen's your home:

By a lake near Jasper a dozen scuba divers
circulated among dripping wooden chairs
set up in the sand.
            "Underwater carpentry"
a bystander explained: each spring
they take mallets and pegs into the lake
to see who can build the best chair.

When I laughed "Strange!"
she flushed and barked "Not *strange!*"
as if I alone had never witnessed
the commonest of rituals.

Leftover pale light gets soaked up
between the buildings, the sponge
of night at work. I wouldn't put night
above day, except for its memory inflood:

Once a boy dreamed of cracking open
a blue-nebula marble — imagining
a galactic swirl of blue stars —
but whacked his thumb with the hammer
so the marble sped away
to be lost forever
under the oil tank — an early chance
to learn how slips, spills, weeds
cropping up out of place and time
gather in the story's heart.

But it's not all a joke:
this may be my last tax-free poem.

Then come the harshest coincidences
beyond laughter: like the night
reading of grieving Tahitian women
scraping their faces with sea shells
   I turned on the news to learn
fourteen young women where I teach
lay broken and still, a gunman frightened
of their new strength, all Saint Cassianus
delusions souring in teachers' mouths.

Wanting the Day

Cartier sighting tiered rock and brush
was headed the right way when he called this
the land God gave Cain —
but what land isn't? A week afterward
we had to give exams, and each time
the elevator doors slid open
I looked out over the young women
bent to their papers, their fingers and hair
touching their necks,
                      the empty doorway
like someone's shadow about to fall.

A door blows shut, a door blows open,
the streets empty as if the barbershop wolf
had sprung to life, only desperate
to find the forest. Does Mrs. Feinstein,
sleepless, reach for her vanished family?

Soon I'll join a lineup for a film
warlike or swallowlike. The street shines
bituminously, but the sky stretches
clear, stars like scattered sparks of the fire
that ate the clothes, limbs, and heart
of William Tyndale.
                    Roped to a pyre
in a town square, the good translator untensed
his fingers one last time. Ploughboy,
take the book in hand.

Underwater Carpentry

A Basement Tale
for Andrew

1

Twin brothers slept on thin cots near a furnace.
One heard a gruff lullaby, a fiery-hearted father;
the other, a smoky-fingered devil sharpening a blade.

With a click and a shudder, the furnace shut off.
For one boy, silence was a shoreless pool rippled
by a single minnow; for the other, a spider,
the tips of eight legs pressed against his face.

Rain slapped the basement windows and seeped in
through cracks — the sky at work feeding rhubarb
in the back yard; the slow growth of mould
over split stones in a Loyalist burial ground.

When the bathroom fan overhead whirred, one brother
heard a whale, fathoms deep, serenading its mate;
the other, an open-mouthed ghost trapped in an iceberg.

2

A click, a shudder — the droning began again.
The twins crawled from bed and slept in the furnace.

One walked into a tropical forest hung heavy with fruit,
shot through with birds spanning the spectrum;
one fell into an inferno that burned up his clothes
and glasses, his eyelashes and lips.

Each brother wrote a book — one with berry juice
and feathers, one with his finger stone-slashed.

3

Upstairs the next day they read each other's words,
baffled. Baffled, curled in back-to-back chairs,
they knit their brows into mazes without threads.

That midnight, back on their hands and knees
they crawled down a trail toward each other's dream
from the crossroads inside the blazing mouth.

An Imp Tale

1

Twin sisters were told never to laugh in church.
Phlegm-throated pigeons on the roof
burbled some service of their own, a young deacon
smelled like he swam in pools of aftershave,
an old woman slurped her gold tooth. But the twins
locked up the imps of laughter, their father's words
like the vaccination scars on their freckled arms.

They fiddled with the hat strings at their throats.

2

That Sunday an out-of-town choir filled the loft,
robed in orange. One sister rolled her eyes, whispered
pumpkins, and her twin coughed. Hunting for high C
a soloist's voice wobbled like that of a lady
slung over a villain's shoulder, shrieking, kicking.

When the silver collection plate slipped, a quarter
raucously rolled across the floor. Their father
grabbed the plate's edge, but not before imps
jumped from their throats. They slapped their hands
to their mouths, to keep the others inside
while the soloist dove into alto.

Who'd tipped the plate? Each was sure she had.
But one felt free; the other, baptized in guilt.

3

During the sermon one sister watched her urchin scurry
like a tiny monkey down the aisle, up the pulpit,
over the gold cross; her memory blurred the fleeing coin
into a rollerskating track down which she sped,
monkeys clinging to her ankles and neck.

Her twin ran over the backs of pews sweeping a net —
the rolling coin a road down which she lurched
dragging a wagon of shame behind her in the dust.

Before the morning of the pumpkin-robed choir
the sisters' straws had shared the same glass.
On the way out, joining hands, they saw their imps
claw and spit at each other in mid-air.

A Drum Tale

1

One winter night a boy became a babysitter
in a bungalow seized and shaken by wind.
Who were they, those neighbours so little like
his parents? In the man's fur-trimmed slippers
he flung his Physics text aside and roamed:

nudes on shower curtains, lascivious-finned
tropical fish, *Provocative Percussion* —
on the record jacket, a great-bellied woman.

Shaking, he slipped the music from its sleeve
by a clay dwarf's lidless eyes and shovel-like penis.

2

In the chimney turbulent snow moaned
You've never seen the sleeper awake . . . awake!
If the baby kicked the wall and wailed
would none of his faltering words chase away
its nightmare? What if it looked *too* asleep,
still as one of the smothered princes
in his father's brittle-paged *Books of Knowledge*,
in the engraving all cold dark blue?

Don't wake . . . don't wake . . .
The elegant curved stereo-arm zigzagged down.

3

He raised his hands, loosened his hips, leapt
between the record-jacket woman's legs
past waterfalls and cliffs to a clearing

where girls lightly skirted in straw danced
his way, closer, closer, imprinting their bare feet
with blossoms and seeds. He muttered *can't stop
moving can't stop moving* — mating time,
his mating dance could win him a wife.

Sweat falling from him like smashed jewellery,
he touched a smooth honeysuckle breast.

4

From the bedroom with the closed door
a voice rose, plaintive, breaking. In the hallway
he still felt an unreined rhythm charging
through him, drums in the background,

but over the blizzard pulling at the eaves
he heard a baby — his own — crying out.
The father in him, fine-veined and afloat, turned.

A Best-Man Tale

1

A best-man forgot the gold studs for his collar.
Fallen to his knees at his brother's feet
he begged forgiveness, then gazed up:
two tiny nails driven into his brother's neck.

While the ushers barked foul names in his ear
his father, scowling, choked him in a headlock
and twisted gold foil through the collar slots.

2

To the best-man all ceremony was death.
The box holding the bride's ring catapulted
from his bony fingers. Later when his cuff
bumped a brimming glass of wine, a red tide rushed
over the shoes of the three hundred guests.

The emcee blared, the heat mounted, video cameras
swivelled — extraterrestrial eyes. His neck swollen
from feasting, the best-man obeyed the order
"waltz with the maid of honour."
Who manacled anchors to his feet?
In his arms, the bride's sister shrank with shame.

3

His Liz or Lou was lost in the crowd.
In their hotel room the night before
they'd rerun old skirmishes, slept without touching.
In the dance-floor swarm of elbows and legs
he found her and smiled. She slapped his face,
the sound a skin drum's stray beat.

Weeping, wandering blocks through the humid night
he knotted his burgundy tie around a lamp post,
waded waist-deep into a fountain pool,
threw the gold studs toward a stone nymph

who took on flesh and opened
her lily-scented arms. The best-man answered
yes, but only if the celebrations
stayed small — no fanfare
but nighthawk cries falling from high above
and a few hidden insects rubbing legs.

A Skater Tale

1

A blind man in despair walked with his dog.
Not even sherry like a swallowed flame,
a many-rivered sonata, or his braille
Bulfinch's Mythology cheered him any more.

From a snowy footbridge a whispery rhythm
slowly grew closer, sharper, a skater circling
a small canal. On the island in the oval
the blind man felt no red-cheeked Mercury darting down
his body's frozen streams,

its winged feet snarls of bone and dust
under the raised script's hard snows.

2

What wild whim did he give in to, following
his dog up the steps of Apollo Sports
where a girl with a peach-soft voice
searched for skates his size? At his back
he sensed skis awaiting fields and woods,
toboggans that had never touched a hill.

Over thick socks, the good fit of new skates
startled him.
        Flight soared to his mind,
promising paths that start at the feet and stretch away,
no horizon waiting to knock him flat, endless space ahead.

3

At midday the mid-city rink lay silent.
He halted, he wavered, he saw himself
a button-eyed scarecrow blown off its perch —
but soon his shoulders and legs recalled it all,
his humming muscles retrieved their buried speeds.
Flying   free   hawk-sure   exultant —

When a fissure tripped him, he staggered
backwards, keeping his head high. Fallen,
he was a spinning X, his bruised elbow a small price.

His dog licked his face with its hot tongue.
It was the sun grown fleshly, telling him
the cradle of old myths swung in his gasping breath.
In his ears, other children of Mercury gathered.

Skylight

The day my cousin shot himself in the head
I was cleaning the skylight in the hall.

The landlady's loose-nailed stepladder
shook with each step I climbed down.
Over the phone my father's voice, 500 miles
away: after a furious standstill
with his wife, my cousin had carried
his cherished inheritance — our grandfather's rifle —
past his sleeping daughter into the back yard.

At the top of the ladder again, I lifted out
the glass. Dead flies, grit, rain smears.
His mother was saying *never talked . . .*
like a shut book.
In our grandfather's hands the rifle
had provided deer meat for his father.

I took the glass to the bathtub for a wash,
jets of Windex, a speedy polishing.
Rare games of crokinole and baseball
had built a flimsy bridge between us.
After its collapse, the time he tried college
I'd glimpse him in the Student Union
shooting pool, game after game. One night
a decade before the end, he was a waiter
in a bar, serving me a beer, silently.

I climbed the ladder a last time to lift
the glass back into place. The hallway
was like a new world. For the first time
I could see sky through the ceiling.
How do we deserve such an inrush,
such clear watery light?

Always

Somewhere a wolf spider dances on a white rock
shaking in fervent frenzy. Somewhere a crippled auk
tries to fly, killdeer mate in a soccer field, a shrike
shoves a warbler onto a thorn. At this moment
a woman watches a meteor, a child counts the seconds
between lightning and thunder, old men share
ale made from malt, hops, and Scottish water.
Always, during your day and during your night
blackflies pierce human skin, rice-shoots
poke through earth, worms tunnel, a mother grazes
her infant's cheek with love for the first time.
Always, heat at the heart of a crematorium is reaching
its peak, and a queen bee drops dead into mud. Pick
any moment: a couple on a mountain inhale air too thin
for their lungs, but feel inexplicably at home,
while a couple wandering through their garden
catch the smells of two dozen species, and feel lifted
into an exotic place. Now, as I write, rain cascades
into a shrunken stream, foxes nip each other,
a rotting peach loses its last firmness. As you read,
a skirt falls to a bedroom floor, tires crush
a crawling animal, fingers press piano keys.
What happens during a pause in your talk
could keep you typing until your last breath. Always
a bullet leaves a gun, honey pours from a spoon.
Your brain is a mussel shell that will never hold the ocean.

Granite Erratics

> To personify *If* — *But* — *And* . . .
> — Hawthorne, *The American Notebooks*

1

If has a tail shaped like a questionmark.
Among meshed branches, it floats from spruce
to pine, pine to birch. The playful one. Furred
with conditionals, its feet twitch even in its sleep.
If *if* weren't with us, the brain might be little more
than a register, the sky a sealed roof.

What if anti-gravity always kept us an inch
off the earth — if frontier artists heard the truth:
    being painted shields you from bullets —
if the curator didn't exaggerate a bit
    when he said "A toad is in heaven
      with a breakfast of earwigs and June bugs" —
if the cat obsessed with reflections speeding up the wall
    leapt, and at its touch light beams became birds.

2

"But," said the wounded, wide-eyed sailor, "but . . .,"
seeing the surgeon pull off his wig and lift out
his own glass eye.
        "But," said the seventy-year-old woman
buried under earthquake rubble, refusing to come out,
"but I'm naked, and people will say I have no shame."

But rears its scaly head, blinks. Now it hisses,
cantankerous; then, makes the mouth's subtlest upturn.
Alert, *But* finds the generous thief, the sour pit
in the sweetness, the lighthouse killing blinded birds.

Wanting the Day

Where would we be without *But*? — under a government
whose voices all huddle into one, on a planet
    without shadows or valleys.

3

And is *And* the greatest of these? Ever-migrant,
at home anywhere, winged and gilled. Eyes bloodshot
with smoke, sea-water, cave-air. Its diseases many, its beauties
contradictory. The generous one. Finds it hard to say *no*.

We have mosses that live 2000 years — a year
and a year and a year — and vireos that sing
20,000 times a day — a song and a song and a song.
We have birds' feet, forgotten by many,
poor cousins to feathers and wings —
                              a grackle's (black)
grasping a wire fence, and a guillemot's (red)
backpaddling, and a willet's (blue) crisscrossing sand.

And crosses the spaces between this and that.
On the coast, step among the granite erratics —
boulders pushed from afar by glaciers
aeons ago, monoliths on wind-flattened plateaus — a rock
and a rock and a rock. Among the haphazard many
each claims a place,
                there, inescapable,
immovable for the meantime.

Granite Erratics

When the Drummer Throws His Sticks Aside
for Don Domanski

He flutters his hands in a microphone —
hummingbird jazz. All surfaces struck,
rubbed and brushed, he slaps his rib cage.

I'd make such music, pull surprises
from surprises. In dense forest silence
a door creaked and I pictured a shack
battered by the seasons, caved in —
then nothing but a bare branch was nudged
by a rhythmical wind. A door swung,
no door swung. Or one cold morning
in a balcony-filled city of millions
someone all clownish floppy white
danced dervish-limbed across a flat roof
until I found it was only chimney smoke
wind-pushed, stretched and shredded.

To show you the fritillary's gilded design
     and its crooked-flying skills!
I won't take you to Sonny's Petting Zoo
where you can stroke a duck's head or tickle
a goat's chin, as if all were declawed,
stuffed with bloodless fabric.
                    I'd shoot the rapids —
but not too fast. Who shoots them the *slowest*,
seeing whirls and thick salmon and flung froth
yet keeping aimed and afloat?

Would that my words bent down and drank water
from a moose track, made bookends
with iron from an abandoned bridge, crossed
the home of mudworms and mussels at low tide
to pick rusted lighters from the sea floor.
In a middle-of-nowhere town, from a bus window,
above a snowy crèche, I saw angels of fishnets.

Wanting the Day

To be fleshed with eloquence
                       like "poor as Job's turkey"
or the signs hammered onto roadside poles
BLIND CREST   OINK MART   NIGHT CRAWLERS
or the phrase on a faded map's pasture
thistle plain and trysting tree.

If I gave all that, you'd feel the freedom
that lightened my legs and shoulders years ago
when a welcome blizzard shut school down
and I walked home
        with the gift of the whole afternoon in my arms,
struggling to breathe, wide-eyed to see,
whipped across my face by a whistling power.

The Uprooted Sleuth

A cigar tossed from a train window hits a cyclist in the eye.
A plot might start there. The sleuth picks up and sniffs
the possible clue. Sounds of his brain at work
drown out the trilling of the toads in the ditch.

He misses the city's chimneys breathing out secrets,
its doorways scarred with crimes. He is ten disguises,
                       a genius of stains, a blade
honed to one purpose. A rook means nothing
deepening its wing-beats above a steeple
unless a bullet in its breast leads to a man
circled in guilt. A spiderweb crossing a shut gate
must prove something: nobody went through.
Moors must be a stage for tragedies,
                       a site for burials.
Why a woman refused to cut her fingernails
intrigues him, but a grebe's fleet mating dance
just beyond the boat in which he scowls
skitters past as far from his mind
as a waterwheel turning in northern China.

When he finds no motives to untangle
like the heap of oily rope curled at his feet,
boredom creeps into his cells.
                       Lonely as a lost moorhen
whose head cannot stop bobbing, he holds a pocket glass
over the cracks and grit speckling his boots. How hard
he hunts for something to make his heart speed up.
Around him trees sink into their own reflections,
chaffinches sing from the hedges of another world.

Needy Space

> . . . *all really inhabited space bears*
> *the essence of the notion of home.*
> — Bachelard, *The Poetics of Space*

He wants to teach classes under the sky.
Hot as a hospital ward, L-201
has all the character of a stripped soup can,
cold tin. Why are the walls blank but for a clock?
In elementary days, paintings made the walls
move — a train with many-faced windows
curving through mountains, a sunflower showering
gold into his eyes. Is a windowless room
any place for learning? Give him a forest clearing,
tree stumps for chairs; a wave-chiselled cove,
air streaming over water and everyone's face.
Does the fool think he's some dryad's son
torn from his native place? *Okay, bow*
to monkish ways, face the faces, voices
and minds that make a place what it is —
Joe shaping answers in the back row,
Jenny in the front. This class has more kick
than any he's coached before — but the room
shaves the five senses, and he secretly
grieves for it. And nothing
he does there is more than a potted
cactus balanced on a podium.

Thanksgiving in an Old House
for Karen

*This holiday is an empty stone well
encircled with rotted leaves. Fill it,
let subterranean streams rush in —*

    for the fuchsia's red blossoms on the sill,
    Indonesian salad, ginger root dissolving
    in our mouths, the nearby siren crying
    how someone would save a life or a house,

for single-celled noctiluca
massed and phosphorescent
on the ocean surface at night,

    for this house of pine planks and old brick
    newly ours, handhewn ceiling beams still
    telling stories of the axemen's swing,

for jumps to the unaxable,
the unphotographable, the unframable,

    for her, the blessing I never expected,
    her voice and hands, all of her, all,

for everything mating our laughter,
optimists "those who say bad weather's
better than no weather at all,"
                    for wind
rubbing our faces when we climb
to a ferry's top deck, in a gannet's wake,

    for the lungs to lament, for all who curse
    a ferry's death and a monster bridge's birth,

for rain on the roof (as long as it won't
leak any more),
                for *as long as, even if,*
yet, still, dashes and parentheses,

    for the Anarchist who gardens,
    the daycare centre in the seniors' manor,
    the keychain skeleton hanging in the hall
    and every other unlikely pairing,

for ingenuity, ingenuity! —
Hearne and his men in 1770 cutting up their tents
for shoes; Muir in Alaska, 1880, scraping shavings
from his sled, tiny kindling to brew tea,

    for all who read closely, all who read
    carelessly (whoever slap-painted the sign
    METHODIST CEMETERY BAKE SALE),
    for *brouhaha, dogsbody, rigmarole, bosky,*

for the bedrock that no done day can be undone,
for regret, so the next game flies fiercer,
for sleep without nightmares, that healer,
that fall into blankness from which we rise
into each other's arms like startled swimmers,

    for the mouth and fingers to give thanks
    and the Zimbabwean thumb-piano, its mighty pluck
    ringing to all the corners of the room . . .

Granite Erratics

The Woods on the Way to School
for Mark Abley

> *When well sheltered, memories are reborn*
> *as rays of being rather than as frozen shapes.*
> — Bachelard, The Poetics of Reverie

A globe in the classroom window marked the end,
   the turning indoors for the morning,
      the afternoon — blue bulb with pale continents

fixed, spied through glass as he rushed
   to the doors, panting, late, his delicious dawdling
      finished. While he leapt over logs and followed

the shadowed path hidden from all houses
   he'd hear the bell clearing the jungle gym,
      pulling him away from the spongy-mossed

ground, the catbird expanding its mimicry,
   the toadstools too flesh-like to touch. Late,
      late. Tardiness x's like birdtracks

crossed the boxes of his attendance record,
   badges of virtue in *his* eyes.
      Through the four seasons of grade four

each morning he walked half a mile downhill
   past shrubs and chimneys and fences,
      then let the thin ragged strip of woods

— a shortcut that slowed him down — swallow him up.
   Full of tricky turns, the path was followed
      by strangers he never saw. Thirty years later

I find nothing but a ghost of those woods, new streets
   in its lap, yet an impossibly familiar tree
      still stands, and from it I try to build

the old space — like staring at a time-bleached
   circus poster on a half-collapsed barn
      until the field flickers with lions and clowns.

How narrow and bounded it all
   must've been, how slight a break
      from marigolds and carports, but for a boy of ten

those trees opened into a wilderness
   rampant with secrets — a dog's skull driftwood clean,
      a clutch of ring-necked-snake babies

writhing. When I read *sylva sacrosancta*
   I think, yes, for one year that was my holy wood.
      Swaying between two times, I sit high in a tree

climbed by nobody else, watching the thin boy
   I once was. It's no fairy tale, but a story
      imprinted in my brain cells deeper than I can go,

in the lines of my hand held up to my face.
   Many days the boy took the trail four times —
      after breakfast, back home at lunch, schoolward

again, homeward at 3 o'clock — so he picked
   his way in all sorts of light, milky, lemony,
      purple. For a month he didn't know

all he was missing, then his first pair of glasses
   brought distant dimnesses closer — birchbark
      with staring slit eyes, a raven's throat

wind-ruffled, snow making skinny saplings
   stalagmites. His father at the supper table
      announced, "If we saw like hawks

Granite Erratics

we could read headlines a quarter-mile away."
    For days he dreamed of having a hawk's eyes
        transplanted into his face, throwing

his glasses away to become some Super Hero
    gifted with the strongest vision on earth.
        Years would grow out of years

before he knew: poisonous mists and liquids
    blurred warblers' voices and loosened
        their feathers' roots, sea turtles mistook

collapsed balloons for jellyfish, swallowed them
    and suffocated. He was cocooned by ignorance,
        an envelope lined with ancient moss.

One morning a ray of light like a Maliseet arrow
    hit the bull's eye on a flat stump —
        a beetle's glittering back. He'd never seen

such luminous blue, like a drop of congealed oil
    or a bit of a stained-glass Jesus robe.
        A fire in his throat woke him that night,

by Sunday he was in the hospital surfacing
    from ether oblivion, his tonsils
        a frog with a bellyful of live coals trapped

at the back of his throat. Bored by the blank
    walls, sore-throated, thirsty, he burrowed
        into a get-well present from his mother,

a shiny-spined book on beetles. What chords
    it struck, what music in the names
        among the quarter of a million kinds —

kangaroo beetle   cucumber beetle
   Hercules beetle   harlequin beetle
      ambrosia beetle   striped blister beetle

rose snout beetle   buffalo-carpet beetle
   Mexican bean beetle   pleasing fungus beetle
      confused flour beetle   twice-stabbed lady beetle

tumbling flower beetle   six-spotted green tiger beetle
   whirligig beetle   devil's coach horses
      — but no beautiful facts would stay with him

except what touched on sexton beetles
   who could've spurred him into praise
      translated: *They do what worms cannot do*

and the beaks of scavengers decline. They work
   for free, send out no catalogues featuring
      mahogany gold-handled coffins. En masse

they can bury a mouse in two or three hours,
   a rat in five or six. Their own limbs and shells
      serving as tools, they plant their eggs

in the flesh of the dead.
   In the hospital room hot as Brazil
      but bare as an Arctic waste, he didn't ask

what I ask, how much the names — *the names —*
   magnetized him. The other day I savoured
      reading *peppered moon lichen, lettuce lung*

lichen, dimpled specklebelly, cryptic paw lichen.
   I remember now, but even then memory
      was a garden or a briar-patch forever crowding

Granite Erratics

side vision. I figure memory must've started
   right after the cradle, even if later chapters
      cancelled the first ones, like weeds

pushing out weeds. At ten, the boy looked back
   at palm trees he'd made rolling up newspapers and
      slitting them from the top, then spraypainting them

silver or green; he uprooted hours when leg aches
   woke him into the middle-of-the-night misery
      of growing too fast. One girl got nosebleeds

every second week or so, red soaking
   the teacher's tissues. The boy kept watching
      on the sly — unsure why — the blood

astonishing among the desks and scribblers
   like his own blood the afternoon he ran
      into a rocky-bottomed lake and hopped ashore

with red gushing down his white foot.
   In a country hospital as a doctor stitched
      the wounded flesh, the boy couldn't forget

the sweet sensation unwinding within the pain,
   the woozy satisfaction knowing his body stored
      such thick brightness. Sex was still an unknown

aurora, a riverbed waiting for water
   to rush in from its brooks, while shapes and sounds
      seduced him everywhere — salamander eggs

like jellied packets of eyes, apple blossoms
   fallen on black mud, a wren's frantic flurried
      meandering higher and higher

Wanting the Day

up the scale. His body a register,
  a taken-for-granted set of clothes. Did he ever
    gaze alone into a mirror? —

a year before a girl touched the curls on his forehead
  leaving a sensation subtle as a light beam
    but strong as if a doe had struck him

with her hoof. Even the time a hard snowball
  shattered between his legs and pain
    rose to his ears and lingered all the way home,

he never thought to look for a bruise, his body
  retreating like a shadow when clouds
    slide over the sun. It was a year when humans

shuffled in the background, signifying less
  than things — as if on a stage
    the painted trees and bushes walked forward

to wave their branches and talk, and the actors
  withdrew into the wings. Yet I know
    differently, I take a spade and unearth

a few faces from the murk . . .
  Everett from down the street disappeared
    one spring night, but by dinnertime the next day

he was back, and neighbours knew he'd hidden
  in the woods, shamed by his report card,
    afraid of his father's wrath. Why did the boy

envy Everett? He was tempted to ask
  how those hours had unfolded — spots of green
    phosphorescence, the very breath of the woods

Granite Erratics

like a brother — but when thunderclouds soon threw
　down darkness deep as an Exodus plague
　　he felt cast into that night: sleepless

wrestling, clammy cold seeping through his shirt,
　the guilty document like a bloody knife
　　in his bookbag, the woods the farthest thing

from home he'd ever known. Then, the day he flung
　a clump of dried mud at a Stop sign
　　to test his arm, or for no more reason

than the pure pleasure of doing it, and a honk
　behind his shoulder announced Sergeant Lawson leaning
　　out a paddy wagon's window to scold and warn,

the lungs of authority hoping to make the small
　quake. I berate myself for saying *Sorry*
　　as if all my cowardly acts since have denied

the delight of watching the mud explode
　like a meteor striking a planet. And I still see —
　　faint as smoke just before it disappears —

the face a girl named Clare brought back to class
　days after her father had jumped off the city bridge
　　carrying his debts and his unreachable secrets,

the grief in her eyes like nothing in the woods.
　With a pencil the boy drew his brain as a factory
　　spewing out paper, an insect-eyed worker stabbing

two dials at once, cogs and wheels turning
　everywhere. Why didn't he sketch
　　his brain as a forest? Were all those machines

Wanting the Day

closer to the truth? Fingerpainting gripped him
   like nothing else in class, he flung himself
      into trays of many colours, all that

unpremediated play shaping lines and ovals
   like branches, roots, and leaves changed
      beyond recognition by the twisting

winds of his feelings. At supper he'd see paint flecks
   under his fingernails like earth clawed
      from the tangled floor of the woods.

A man walking miles from any house or road
   picks up an oak leaf fallen from its twig
      and sees in its veins and clinging wet

a long pocket of trees from thirty years ago,
   the pocket with a hole that emptied him
      into a schoolyard, above a hard-to-believe

globe in a window. Through every forest he finds
   the trail that followed him from his tenth year
      into his eleventh. In a foot-sized pool

rimmed with cones and pods, in the depths
   of a wasp nest like an abandoned clay headdress,
      through a bullet hole in a *No Trespassing* sign

he sees the year he first knew he was
   spellbound, when he detoured from the street
      into a land of blue beetles and moss.

A Sliver of Dawn

Did I open one eye, both, neither? When wind
knocked a blind's cord against a sill, a jay
shrieked in the garden. Ten seconds or so of waking,
then sleep pulled me back down by both legs.

I can't recover much except that voice
livid in the lilacs or the maple — a raw cheer,
                        an alarm, a life-blood call
that might've sprung from my own throat.
No chorus of ten species sends higher waves
through the air. I grasped sound like an outfielder leaping
to a high fly, then sank back into sleep
                        empty-handed.

The many-roomed cave of dreams gives us
other eyes and ears. Its fears end
with miraculous suddenness, unlike ones we live with
all day. But as far as I know, I've never heard a jay
in there. What I've not witnessed during sleep
could take years just to tell — mating blue-black
dragonflies rasping and vibrating
on a peony bush, an eclipse that made the air
a blurred furriness, an Indian rubber ball
streaking down a street with nobody in sight . . .

From sleep's deeper caves I might offer
a different report. But this morning
I felt closer to home when a jay
cracked the air, and for a few moments
  — muddled, struggling — I wanted the day.

Under the Old Roof

All day, light rubbed and streamed over everything on shore
    but other than noting
overriding blue, I hardly gave the sky a thought.
    Far past midnight
when I slid from sleep and out of the tent,
    the star-jammed
blackness nearly threw me on my back. Then the sky
    was the one thing
to watch, like a billion acres of voices and signals
    demanding attention,
more than any shivering man could do. Had I ever been
    so awake? —
yet I couldn't answer *hey you, you, you, you, you*
    all at once. My eyes
filled up with brightnesses flung from farther
    than I'll ever go.

I recalled an Italian count, some novel's sullen brooder,
    dubbing the sky
"old roof," saying our sins had plastered it with centuries
    of gloom,
and I knew all kinds of our junk ripped and zipped past
    out there.
Still, imprinted with the day, I searched for constellations
    never named —
Seal, Tern, Heron, Sandpiper — and felt the sky was some
    limitless mind
dancing, or a sea of secrets suddenly breaking through.

*

Under the taken-for-granted blue
the first seal surfacing
had seemed a stranger wading ashore

after days hugging flotsam,
forehead masked in black hair.

Glistening amidst
many glistenings, sleekness
complete, two others
lifted their heads, bobbed and
stared, stared and bobbed —
"like beings off a U.F.O."
I thought at the tide's edge
but they could've barked
   What's your business, alien
   glaring at us? What world of little hair
   have you travelled from?

Above the driftwood line, a toad
sluggishly hopped
across leafy mulch, then
went still, so intent on camouflage
I felt a pinprick of guilt
just watching, scribbling
mental notes on his ridges and lumps.
When he inched under
greater safety, my boot nudged
aside the bleached board,
robbing him of cover.

He raised no frightened eyes
to me, who might've been
a tall monstrosity to him
(or merely useless
like a bathing suit to a seal,
a flashlight to the stars).

*

Where 3 a.m. blackness swallowed the beach
I couldn't find one new constellation
among the neck-spraining masses of stars.

Back in the tent, the day's creatures
gathered around the balled-up jacket of my pillow.
A double darkness of night and tent
encased me
          yet dragonfly and bloodworm and heron
darted, burrowed, and stalked in the sides
of my side vision, each a tangle of urges and cells.
On the edge of sleep
three pairs of eyes glistened among waves.

The Afterlife of Trees
for Don McKay

Neither sheep nor cows crisscross our lives as much.
Trees dangle apples and nuts for the hungry, throw
shade down for lovers, mark sites for the lost,
and first and last are
utterly themselves,
fuller and finer than any number or letter,
any 7 or T. Their fragmentary afterlife goes on
in a guitar's body and a hockey stick, in the beaked faces
up a totem pole and the stake through a vampire's heart,
in a fragrant cheeseboard, a Welsh love-spoon,
a sweat-stained axe handle, a giant green dragonfly
suspended from the ceiling with twine,
in the spellbinding shapechanging
behind a glass woodstove-door . . .

and in a table I sanded and finished this week.
— *Finished?* — Four grades of sandpaper drew out
alder's "nature," inimitable amoeba shapes,
waves, half moons, paw prints dissolving in mud.
What looks more beautiful after death? We sand
and sand, but under the stain, beyond our pottery
and books, our fallen hairs trapped in the varnish,
something remains like memories of a buck
rubbing its horns on bark. Soaked in
deeper than the grain goes: cries, whistles, hoots.

A Toss of Cones

Twelve months, and one more ring to the tree —
a measurement of years, hidden as our marrow.
Show me a table that grows like that.

No alder chair lets leaves go in October
and unfolds others in May. No birch garden-stake
twists to left or right, thirsty for sunlight.
A bird's-eye-maple bowl doesn't throw
many-branched shadows over the ground
any more than ashes broadcast on the wind
are a man or woman remembered and mourned.

Don't talk to me about the afterlife of trees.
I need places where sap drops in a bucket
and jack pines start up through fire-blackened soil,

where wingseeds spin down through air, a toss
of cones on the orange earth.

In a minute you can walk — for now,
you can walk — from dim woods where firs
squeeze out other firs,
                        to a lone butternut tree on a riverbank
spreading its limbs like an embrace of the air.

After breathing paper too long, be glad to know
a white elm drinks fifteen hundred gallons of water
from a hot dawn to a hot dusk

and Moroccan goats climb to the highest branches
                              of argan trees
to eat the sweet leaves and bark.

Sloth Surprises

> *Like a rainbow before breakfast, a sloth is a surprise,*
> *an unexpected fellow breather of the air of our planet.*
> *No one could prophesy a sloth.*
> — William Beebe, *Jungle Days*

How would you feel hanging in cecropia trees
    until algae slicks your fur? Would you flinch
at being called a termite nest, a doormat draped

    around a branch, the mop-head butt of naturalist jokes?
("a masterpiece of immobility..." "an enthusiasm for life
    excelled by a healthy sunflower...

the second hand of a watch often covers
    more distance"). And what flips and flops
would your ego do if you were named in honour

    of a Deadly Sin? Its Spanish nickname:
Perico Ligero (Nimble Peter), better praise than *Sloth*.
    Lethargy and listlessness are all

many think of it, lazily. Even a sloth Web site
    (yes, there are a few) kicks off with comedy:
the William Tell Overture galloping

    from Packard Bell speakers. Pointing out
they sleep eighteen hours a day is like announcing
    dolphins leap, wolves howl, and gulls

tear garbage apart. What I want is what
    shakes up the known. Give me
the sport of snails, the mourning of sparrows,

      the rage of porcupines. I'm still waiting
to hear the worm that sings. Though no giraffe,
          the sloth could boast (if it chose to) the most

neck vertebrae of any mammal, the greatest range
          of temperatures. Caterpillars in its algae-matted coat
become moths that sip water from its nostrils and eyes.

      "Life disputes with death every inch of flesh . . .
I saw the heart of one beat for half an hour
          after it was taken out of the body."

And it swims, how it swims! When the Amazon
          rises higher, sloths cross a mile underwater
in no time, swinging their long forelimbs one

      after the other, blending dexterity and force.
Destined for other trees and camouflage,
          their hearts pick up speed, their great claws

cut water spangled with startled fish. All
          associations of sin wash from their thick fur.
Sloths swim with the might of eagles flying.

The Afterlife of Trees

From *Talking to the Birds*

> ... one's cry of O Jerusalem becomes little by little
> a cry to something a little nearer and nearer until
> at last one cries out to a living name, a living place,
> a living thing.
>
> — Wallace Stevens, *Opus Posthumous*

1. *to a red-eyed vireo*

Minimalist of the tree tops,
more than a scrap of the dawn chorus, all day
you ask and answer one question
in two-to-four-note phrases, your drawl's inflections
reversing, a rise giving way to a fall, a fall
to a rise,
       ask, answer,
                ask, answer ...
Is it fair to say you sound like a lecturer who won't
move on to the next point,
                or some weary barker
slowly going mad with the monotony of selling?

"*Vireo* is Latin for *I am green*," I can say,
"your back is olive, your cap grey, you raise cowbirds
who squirmed and pushed your nestlings
to their deaths" —
                but how can I pretend to know
what you ask and answer? Or even
that you ask and answer anything?

From the highest leaf-hidden branches
your voice wriggles into my ear, turns more nerve-
rattling than any scream or shriek. If I blocked out

Wanting the Day

all the other notes in the woods and listened
only to yours, all day, every day, I might be the one
who slipped into the shadows forever

repeating the one thought I can't give up.

2. *to a northern gannet*

Fog like cold sweat coated every inch of the ferry,
swathed and hid the ocean ten feet out. Downstairs
indoors, passengers snacked, napped,
fought the warriors and demons of video games.

For those of us circling the deck
the first hour of the crossing didn't yield
one bird, one mewl or wayward cry. Grand Manan
could've been a mile off, or a thousand.
If allowed extravagance, I'd say
the waves peaked and toppled like the waves
                             in the story of the seven days
when "everything according to its kind"
was born. Then, you:
                        flying, unmistakable, goose-sized,
your butter-yellow head the one contrast
to all that pallor. Where everything else was wispy
and smudged, you were suddenness, otherness,
completeness,
eyes and beak and wingbeat.

Just as quickly, you slipped back behind
the gathering of spectres. When I pushed closer
against the cold iron railing
                          you were back with me,
then vanished again, like a feeling that keeps coming
and going on the verge of sleep.
For a minute you were the first bird, or the last.

5. *to a goldfinch*

That is not you. It's a stuffed effigy. The deep
undulations of your flight were finished
decades ago. In the old glass cabinet, the silence
never ends. Wild canary, you no longer shake
thistledown to the earth, no longer sing
your descending notes as you follow your rolling
route through the air. That's not you, but a body
drained of blood — paralyzed force, gesture
without motion — the colour of withered dandelions
squeezed dry. For you I remember
bits of saints filling a vast room in Italy —
blackened anklebones, twisted fingerbones,
so-and-so's kneecap done forever with kneeling.
Around the body you once filled, others are pinned
in clusterings you never knew. At your shoulder
the tanager's scarlet is anemic; at your claws
the bunting's blue is faded and peppery.
This June morning, maybe, a descendent of yours
generations down the line
climbs and dips, moving gold, over a meadow.

8. to a sooty shearwater

You look like a chimney swift who can't find his way home
but this *is* your home. "Water, water everywhere" is your terra

firma, your eyes alighting on land less than ours
on water. Beyond nesting season, only the wildest winds

drive you ashore. If your colour's dull, your flight's not:
a few quick wingbeats, then gliding low over everchanging waves

steady but shifting to the watery heaving, so close that it
sprinkles your feathers, or your wings slice it

in passing. What if some land bird always skimmed
that close to earth, ruffling grasses but never crashing

against rock or wood? Resting, you pick shrimp
from a crest, a trough. More quick beats — off

you glide again, wave-glancer, locomotion expert, quiet
but for a rare lambish cry. For landlubbers at sea, *out there*

turns into *out here*, but our minds aren't big enough
to know your days as you know them, minute

to minute, flying through them, inches over breaking waves.

A Lake Named After My Ancestors

I haven't seen it in years. Even then the iron tracks
on the overlooking ridge seemed forever silent.
The sun was the only train that warmed the rails.
I would walk between the rusted lines, over
the split ties, and never hear rumbles or whistles
announcing imminence. Below, a lake not much bigger
than a baseball field, a spattering of white water lilies
at one end, spruce hemming the water in.

I can't recall otters' backs shining, mergansers
surfacing; no makeshift raft or oil patch
inched between the shores. Despite the lake's plainness,
with my first camera I caught something of it
and framed an enlargement — a Father's Day present.
I wish I could list splendours of the lake named
after my ancestors — a craggy island, light
tinting the blue water purple, boulders
like stepping stones to an underwater paradise —
but I remember an unpopulated blankness
as if it were awaiting settlement
and meaning, locked in a time when the land
was young as egg and sperm.

I never measured its depths, and have no
stories to tell about it. What did my father think
when he absentmindedly glanced at it
above his pens and envelopes? "If not for my name,
it would be nothing"? On those tracks I was distant
and dry, no more real than the no-see-ums
that must've made shattered haloes over the water,
the breeding, big-throated frogs I'm guessing
were there. Why, just once, didn't I scramble
down the ridge and plunge in?

After the Age of Parties

So slowly has he crept into middle age
he can't pinpoint when the parties of his youth
became distant and dreamlike, reflections
on rain-smeared windows. It was in another city
he lived alone through his twenties, gathering
odd jobs like a collector of postponed futures,
cycling through dangerous streets with few thoughts
of danger, tending nothing but cacti in small apartments.

When the smell of spring mud rose from alleyways
and invaded balconies, or when snow puddled
by boots at the door, he improvised zigzag courses
among friends and strangers, eyeing happiness
as explorers eye mountaintops from level land.
In a fiddler's kitchen, he played the spoons until two Irishmen
mocked his rhythms. Later at a Greek bodega, backed
into a corner with no easy exit, he walked across the table
past candles and jugs of sangria, and a waiter threatened
to throw him out. Some nights in murky dining rooms
near furniture hulked like shapes in catacombs
he danced until his glasses slipped down his nose,
hair sweat-jagged. One such night he laughed
at a rich girl gathering her empties to take home
so her dad could cash them in, and she lashed out,
"Nosy bastard!" Stung, he retreated to the balcony;
a voice from a car jeered, "*Sautez, mon ami!*"

He saw himself as a Beast with no Beauty;
a skulking, timid tom in a pack of cats.
Some nights when he walked home, sirens shrieked
their melodrama over rats' tails of drenched grass.
Uniformed doormen he glimpsed through glass
were statues he wanted to smash. Women's faces

were already filling up his memory,
the forests of their hair waving.

In a smaller city, as he drops another log
into his wood stove and reads a book about dragons
to his daughters,
                        laughter out on the street
hints at those nights when the great city
spiralled into his eyes, and he tried a drink called
Moscow Mule, and he felt a ridiculous triumph
on his doorstep, dazed and lonely, finding the right key.

Parties that flickered with hope often ended
with wishes for healing oblivion. Yet he catches
a bit, a spark — faded but glowing — of nights
whirlwinds scattered promises around his feet
while taxis nosed their way through labyrinths
and headlights shone on the mountain like comets.

Every Lion Until Now

Every lion until now was sun-faced, lacy-maned,
a Leo with beaming eyes and no hint of claws.
A child who first walked ten months ago
learns the word "dark," giving the "d" and the "k"
their full force. Now he says "lion"
with his voice shaking, his lip lowered
in fear, and the lion and the dark go together.

He sees a beast in the unlit confusion below
the basement stairs, under the rocking chair
by his costume box, in the shadowed
distances of the study. His parents can't say
how the soft-pawed creature changed overnight
any more than how the first manticore stalked
through a mind thousands of years ago.
Maybe one day the child looked into a mirror
and saw the darkness behind his own teeth;
maybe all of a sudden he heard
the danger in his own comical roar. Fear
is more than a taste he doesn't like,
more than a strategy to get his way. Weeks ago
the first slap of ocean waves against his legs
made him whimper and ask to be held.

The father thinks: *The dark needs a body,
the lion serves the purpose.* It seems some maw
opens and opens and would swallow
all — boy, room, house. When their son runs
to their legs, the parents look into the obscurity
he shows them, and they glimpse again
the breeding cave of their own dread,
a source nothing on earth lights up.

The Afterlife of Trees

A Glosa for Joshua

> *You will come to a place where the streets are not marked.*
> *Some windows are lighted. But mostly they're darked.*
> *A place you could sprain both your elbow and chin!*
> *Do you dare to stay out? Do you dare to go in?*
>   — Dr. Seuss, *Oh, The Places You'll Go!*

I've waited two years to write you some lines
— nothing you'll read for a very long time.
Past midnight I picture you wrestling these words
at twelve or twenty, when you might ask the page,
"Who were you talking to when I was just two?"
One day when you ask what it would've been like
if the land were the ocean and the ocean the land,
if your mother and I never boarded one boat,
if the dogfish all meowed and the catfish all barked,
you will come to a place where the streets are not marked.

Riddles of the what-if and the never-was
crawl in from the sea like Edinburgh mist,
mist of the castled city where we first gave you
a chance to be. To imagine you now as not
is to face a blank like no other blank,
to pause and stumble, bereft and shocked.
When we lead ourselves by the nose into dreams
that this or that never was — candles, mirrors,
hopes, regrets, the red-throated loon, the great auk —
some windows are lighted. But mostly they're darked,

Wanting the Day

and if we stand there too long we grow cold.
When you're forty-something, my age tonight,
will I be a scattering of ashes? — (taboo:
father hints of his own X). Near the harbour shops,
where you call a lobster trap and a dreamcatcher
basketball nets, we see one boat named VIM,
one named VIGOUR. Some day we'll learn
to laugh at the grave and trip up ogres
by making bad jokes, like calling a coffin
a place you could sprain both your elbow and chin.

The child you are and the man you will be
blend into each other, back and forth
— back and forth, the child you are and the infant
you were. The first morning that rises without me
will be bright compared to your never having been.
In Scotland there was a b & b, and in the b & b
your mother and I imagined a door, and on the door
your face was sketched in invisible ink. That night
we entered and left in the dust the questions
"Do you dare to stay out? Do you dare to go in?"

The Afterlife of Trees

Sick for the New Millennium
December 31, 1999 – January 1, 2000

A man overcome with raw throat, backache,
feverish cheeks and forehead
clung to home and felt like doing nothing.
Each trip down to the kitchen
like a child learning stairs
he gripped the bannister with one hand.

As year folded into year, with blankets to his chin
he watched torches tossed high in New Zealand,
waltzes spun in the streets of Vienna, mallet music
hammered between ice walls above the Arctic Circle.
Fireworks chainlinked China — Paris —
London — the Grand Parade a mile from his couch.
Did he want to be out there? He couldn't say
for sure — but when strangers in far-flung cities pointed
microphones at shrieking crowds and asked,
"Having *funnnn?*" he almost bit his blankets.

Red-nosed, he pressed his face to a window
above the back yard: no celebrating flowers sprung up
out of season, no beasts strayed from the woods
to watch explosions and sniff the sizzled air.
The trees stood there as usual, changing
imperceptibly, no calendars in their branches.

In bed he thought of his son, new to speech,
chanting excitedly, "One two eight six!"
Once numbers had charmed him too
with their novelty, useful for pigs, balloons, and blocks

Wanting the Day

but not yet for years, whatever years were
(the days more than enough).

Reaching through the dark for his glass of water,
he wished this night were to him as it was
to the mice in the walls, the whales off the coast —
a time unique as any; yet he was trapped
in a world of counting, where years are added up
like spoons and fingers and pages. Until he slept
he felt numbers falling upon him,
falling upon him
like a whisper of data, a dark blizzard of ashes.

Lost Footnote from an Essay on Rhythm

*after watching four Buster Keaton
movies in one weekend*

Walking dulls a pinch in the shoulders, sharpens a thought
    in the mind — tells me the measure is right,
the machine running smooth. On days rare as lightning, a different urge

    pulls me up like wind from the back:
I would run with lungs of limitless air, speed
    down streets with no time to read their names,

spring over walls and shrubs with breath-giving grace.
    While I walk, light-sneakered, I watch another
break from my blood and run:

    finding the cheetah or Keaton within, he stops traffic
as if danger didn't exist, leaps through an open window
    and out an open door, splashes through a stream

like a horse unstrapped from harness and work, inhales
    and exhales up a hill and down,
starts a rockslide that sends boulders bounding past

    his shoulders. He doesn't care if anyone —
a gang of cops or howling children, the hound of heaven —
    chases him. Neither escape nor search,

the race is all muscle thrill and blood surge,
    going back to the day a Cro-Magnon first
laughed because he could run for no reason.

    When he's dashed, swerved, and flown for hours,
a raindrop-simple thought falls:
    in a place I can hardly recall, a deep chair

waits with a footstool and a full glass.
     But for a minute more he knows
fence-leaping freedom, heart-charging nimbleness,

a spring gushing, unstoppable, along the earth —

Foot-doctor for the Homeless

Day after day, I see more toenails than eyes.
I'd push the truth if I said my office
is smaller than my patients' cardboard shelters,
but it's more cramped than most. The floor tiles curl
at the edges, the light bulbs are bare, and Hank
might hear Horace's cracking joints behind the screen.
Only a few old men call me "Ma'am," like I was
a teacher from their childhoods more distant
than death.
            Years ago when the devils of arthritis started
needling my feet, I withdrew from General Practice,
learned everything I could about ankles, heels, shins,
the metatarsal and the phalanges, the way a rabbi
dissects Deuteronomy. I've unknotted laces
that fell apart like spaghetti, peeled off
running shoes that erupted like abscesses.

More than shirts or hats, shoes tells stories —
of chafings and stumbles, a thousand weathers,
a schizophrenic's circular miles trod,
trod, trod. Famous footwear — Cinderella's,
Chaplin's — are odourless in the face of the real.
I've seen no feet I would dry with my hair.
They're the colour of mushrooms, wilted roses,
eggplant skin. Hands rubber-gloved, I swear
feet have voices, words arising from blisters
and broken flesh, not from mouths and beards.
Those voices tell me, mumbling or unexpectedly
clear, raspy or childlike, of frostbitten nights in parks,
skinhead stormtrooper boots, a door forced shut
where the clean and moneyed are wanted.

When the feet twitch with monologues, I can't get a word
in edgewise against the jagged curses and

laughter, all entangled with enemies and wraiths.
Then I feel like some doctor in hell, a fire
burning at my door. The poor and the miserable
were cast there not for punishment, but merely
by the whims of whatever does the casting.

Some nights at home, I stare at my feet
projecting beyond the tub's foam: afflicted
but lucky. Back on the street, the homeless might hobble
less, but trailing my fingers in lavender oil I ask
who will bandage their minds, who will pour ointment
onto their nerves? When I write out slips
for the pharmacy or the hospital, I'm never sure if
they'll reach other hands, or flutter down the sidewalk
in a wet wind. As I pull the plug of my bath,
I've pictured my prescriptions and referrals,
like prayers ending mid-sentence, sluiced away
                              in the street's rain.

The Sonographer
for Al Moritz

Call me Broadcaster of the Early Heartbeat,
First Examiner of the Head's Circumference,
He Who Sees Your Child First. Call me
young Mr. Faith, Mr. Hope. I could say:
"high-frequency sound waves going at
five-to-seven million cycles per second."
A fine science, this. Most days it's business
as usual; but when the commonness of it all
subsides, for a few seconds it seems — dare I say —
sacramental, and I recall holding my wife's hand,
watching our son turn like a shadowy fish
on the screen (not "ghostly form,"
ghostliness being on the other side of life).

I'm the coroner's sunny double, his lucky brother.
Just once, I'd have us switch places
to spare him dark questions and bloody probings
for a night. I wonder if he'd bow
to the consummate promise of a fetus forming —
if he'd weep to be in my shoes.

Vacationing, I get hungry for the moment
when a shoulder or foot comes into view,
the opposite of dissolving. It gets addictive, this gentle
saying to strangers, "There it is — see?"
Once I sat all week on a Cuban beach with the sky
like an empty screen, and I would've been glad
to see a cloud as small as a kneecap.

The news, of course, isn't always cheering. Then
what I see straightens my mouth, tightens a knot
in my throat. I've jotted symbols you don't want
to grasp, but Drs. MacKeigan or Varma or Finch
deliver the news. I see, and say nothing, guilty

I'm spared the job. I've seen celebration drain
from eyes in an instant, then a week later
struggle back, stubborn, giving a welcome at last.
"Sweet one," they whisper, ". . . angel."

Who can *see* hope more clearly than I, day
after day? — a shadowy head turning this way,
a thumb going to a mouth, like a joke
at our gazing, our impatience. I'm one of fate's
surveyors. Maybe it's a right no one
should have — to be an eavesdropper on the future,
always the first on board to spot
a thin beautiful line of land barely lifting
                              above the horizon and the sea.

How Acupuncture Is Like Poetry

The end of my tongue tingles from the needle in my chest.

Listening on the Back Steps

You're glad when one word from your keyboard
startles you. Some days even more than that
works out, then you stand back
                     to see what you've made:
a box for small births, wings fluttering
under the roof. So you've managed to offer
some grubs, and a home of waterproof wood.

But whenever you read those whose words
surround you like a new kind of weather,
you see who you are:

you're the one who climbs out the window
                     while his parents sleep
and walks many blocks to where the music is played —
the Panama, Greenleaf Gardens, the Novelty Club.
Too young to get in, you haunt the back steps
craning toward a door propped open with a brick
until your ears hum and burn. Your heart quickens
when you hear a sound rise above the others,
         its slow fat notes,
                fast agile ones,
the shocks of unexpected accents.

Home with your sax, hungry to learn, you practice
at dawn, noon, dusk. Years pass like hastily scanned
bars of notes. No matter how much you make
some corner of your neighbourhood sing,
you know you'll never leave those steps —

short-breathed, hunched, listening to that voice
burst through the doorway and float through the night
and swing open whatever is shut, whatever needs more air.

Author's Note

This selection represents three decades of work and play in poetry, from 1971 to 2001. Changes have been made in many poems since their first book publication. The poems are arranged to reflect the sequence of their original collections, but I've experimented with the order of poems within collections, giving the poems new neighbours. Many other patterns are possible. I've gained a better appreciation of musicians shuffling their song lists rather than just repeating the previous night's order.

More friends than I can mention have encouraged, coached, advised, and inspired. Thanks to the editors of New Brunswick Chapbooks, Villeneuve Publications, Goose Lane Editions, Ekstasis Editions, and McGill-Queen's University Press. All poems from *The Afterlife of Trees* are reprinted with permission of McGill-Queen's. Thanks also to all the editors who originally wanted these poems, often in older versions, for their periodicals: *The Antigonish Review, Arc, Canadian Literature, Event, The Fiddlehead, The Globe and Mail, Grain, The Malahat Review, Montreal Writers' Forum, Officers' Quarterly, Poetry Canada Review, Pottersfield Portfolio, Prism International, Quarry, Queens' Quarterly, The New Brunswick Reader, Windhorse Review, Writers' Forum* (England), *Zymergy*; and for their anthologies: *Ninety Seasons* (1974), *Cross/cut* (1982), *Easterly* (1983), *The Lyric Paragraph* (1987), *The Landscape of Craft* (1990), *Fiddlehead Gold* (1995), *We All Begin in a Little Magazine* (1998), *Home for Christmas* (1999), *Losers First* (1999), *I Want to Be the Poet of Your Kneecaps* (1999), *Meltwater* (1999), *Following the Plough* (2000), *New Canadian Poetry* (2000), *Landmarks* (2001), *Coastlines* (2002). "Underwater Carpentry" won the 1991 *Malahat Review* Long Poem prize, and "Foot-doctor for the Homeless" won first prize in the 2000 Petra Kenney Awards.

The translation from Kazantzakis in one poem's epigraph is by Temi and Theodora Vasils; and those from Bachelard are by Etienne Gilson and Daniel Russell. The quotations in the "Sloth Surprises" are from Lorus J. and Margery J. Milne, *Marvels and Mysteries of Our Animal World* (1964); William Beebe, *Jungle Days* (1923); and Charles Waterton, *Wanderings in South America* (1825).

Thanks also to the Canada Council for the Arts, the Banff Centre for the Arts, the Hawthornden Castle International Retreat for Writers, and Saint Mary's University. Special gratitude to Morgan Kenney, who opened the gate for me to meet Harry Chambers of Peterloo Poets, Cornwall, England; to Harry, for first suggesting this book; and to Susanne Alexander and Laurel Boone, for suggesting a Canadian edition and seeing it through with such dedication.